Tarot Card Notebooks

Made in United States
North Haven, CT
11 January 2025

64296365R00083